T0273346

The Girl Who Became a Rabbit

the Girl who Became a Rabbit

Emilie Menzel

HUB CITY PRESS
SPARTANBURG, SC

Book design: Kate McMullen
Cover Image: Anne Siems
Cover Text: Julie Jarema
Author Photo: Sean T. Bailey

TEXT: Bell MT

Library of Congress Cataloging-in-Publication Data

Names: Menzel, Emilie, 1992- author.
Title: The girl who became a rabbit / Emilie Menzel.
Description: Spartanburg, SC: Hub City Press, 2024.
Identifiers: LCCN 2024011618 (print)
LCCN 2024011619 (ebook)
ISBN 9798885740371 (trade paperback)
 ISBN 9798885740425 (epub)
Subjects: LCGFT: Prose poems.
Classification: LCC PS3613.E55 G57 2024 (print)
LCC PS3613.E55 (ebook)
DDC 811/.6--dc23/eng/20240325
LC record available at https://lccn.loc.gov/2024011618
LC ebook record available at https://lccn.loc.gov/2024011619

Hub City Press gratefully acknowledges support from the National Endowment for the Arts, the Amazon Literary Partnership, Chapman Cultural Center, and the South Carolina Arts Commission.

HUB CITY PRESS
200 Ezell Street
Spartanburg, SC 29306
1.864.577.9349

"To build a house: one is for shelter,
the other to unfold, and in the
distance is the difference between
sunlight in a field and the lesser
seen light of the other sky."

—Jennifer S. Cheng

in the garden widely
I was a rabbit gathering
my whiskers holding dew on my morning
a trembling coat

full of air a young boy
in the morning in a cap
I unexpectedly saw my excitement
was still there during my afternoon

finding breakfast of wilderness
by a lettuce leaf which I explored
do others the wide roots
hold a propensity of a favorite

for trembling willow tree
I wonder the day dark now
I return and have been marked
to my lettuce leaf as returned

the morning to the garden
was good where I will sleep
and I was observed by the mushrooms
wandering for the evening

1

To speak the haunting, let the body be seen through the trees, and the trees through the body, and the body not be seen at all. Tree branch grief. Wind bristle grief. Giddy with sun reminded of ghost. It was collaring; I could not cage it. It was lowing; I could not speak it. What is to speak and to speak of it forming, the moving it forward, the living as child, the skin still redreaming? The sheep through the trees, seen rough but not fully. Seen bright but not fully. Seen clean. Seen alone.

I have been complicit in slant panes of light. He tips me with light that fills me with dust, calls air a containment to gather our arches. To speak whole the room let the room speak of you. We stand the room hips, my small breasting hips, practice our angling to keep the room centered. Tip me with light to till me with light. To yearn me be animal, I yearn to be animal. At least when you're animal, you know you are loved.

We are all of our versions: the sick and the languid, juxtapositions of the mundane, the pain of budding shoulders blooming like antlers from our backs, thin scoops of bone growing us into a creature when a creature is safest, is distanced enough to be a fabled enactment of me. I start my swan creature unfolding, the arms loosening arcing, the cicadas now suckling, the borrowed skin climbing, moving away from the embrace of the head.

If the it of the body was decided by an us, how much did we lose in losing one another? How much of the world played out in my head when I wasn't looking, and is that what we call complicity? I built a body like I built a home—to keep the other out. If I wrap my sheets around me in hiding, do I grow white wings, can I loop my crane neck under my wing, wrapped neatly like a hose, she dribbles water.

Sometimes she is a leaky sea that must be drained, unplugged and emptied. This is not a body in pain. This is a body more victorious. The story of a selkie slipping in and out of her skins. Silhouette remolded. Dance as an assembly of human geographies.

Sometimes it happens that our bodies receive us in confusion, that the whittler who carves us pulls the knife when he shouldn't, that we end up stringed like unkind violins. And a body shouldn't have to stay as a body does not want to be. Navigate new skin, find thread against bone. Let the imagined body be more important than the real.

It is a funny thing to realize we have been carrying a creature in our pockets unknown for years. Look at our hands. Look at our fingers. Consider how we curl our body how every day we curl our own body into a shell. The snail is our curled fist or our curled fist is a snail, and in our curling we realize we and our creature need one another, that the imagined requires resources of the real and the real requires materialization of the imagined.

In mornings, I must acknowledge my shadow or spend the day in darkness. My shadow and I rise together. My shadow rolls a tantrum on the floor and I step over her to retrieve my coffee. When I dress, I slip her on like silk stockings, but we both know she's no luxury. She winds her way up my legs. We pass the day dragging one another through dirt and our skin the sites of many small dramas. Returning home, we've at least accrued experience. I untangle her from my torso so she can wander the house while I sleep. Let her shadow color fully formed spend the night bleeding out into the corners of rooms. Early morning, let her return to bed, exhausted, curl into us under the covers of our home.

I am trying to rebuild a soft home in soft light, the way a family fills with light breathing and can easily, after dinner, hold together in quiet. To be safely lonely is a feeling I am closer to than to be safely together. I curl, and I am trying to be bigger but my body is a body and must grieve for emotions, and a body in grieving is sloppy and turning and does not sleep without flaring and I want to know that you, too, are feeling, not as punishment, but as recognition that we were once tethered.

We are a body relearning how to navigate the world as only one body. We will fable the body to give it beginnings. Our mother built us a spine. We rolled octagons into our hands while wheeling piano scales. We discovered our arms while climbing trees. It's doing things hands do. It's doing things cross faced. It's living a world where pockets are mammals and milk is a cheapening and we all are a whole collection of other. Unrobe our shape behavior to skin our cheeks. Unfurl a leaky sea to leaky light, I open a window and let—

2

In our backyard, there is a remembered and reliable fig tree. We watch as the macaques climb the branches like children pulling up their mother's arms. The fig tree's head is dark green and slant leafed. The macaques' fur glows brown in the ease of the sun. The macaques tangle up the tree to shake down figs for the younger macaque climbers still navigating the ground. A fig can be eaten in only one handful. Macaques are particular about the ripeness of their fruit, though maybe not as particular as orangutans would be. See the plumped pink macaque cheeks, the pink palmed macaque feet, with nails, scratched fig tree tree bark, the fig tree reliable and marked and so staying remembered.

Our father tells a story at dinner about how he still feels guilty for a time in middle school when he accepted a ride home from the town milkman on the town milkman's electric scooter. It goes like this: he gets dropped off at his house front door and he bounds inside, and his mother suspiciously says to him *now you're home quick and he says back quite sincerely sure am got a ride!* Now his mother's irritated and now his mother's a bit livid and now his mother's explaining that motorcycles are dangerous and rides from strangers are dangerous and what the hell was he thinking. He as an adult expresses shame for as a pre-teen talking back to his mother: *the ride was just there it was only just there and I didn't mean anything by it.* Our father could make his mother so mad so mad sometimes he'd deserve a quick slap.

If I leave the apartment for the day, the furniture still sits there. The frames still hold the walls. I've spent a lifetime crafting a conception of home and here I've come to rest. Green papered flowers. Blue suede chair. Tell me the story. Now tell me again. If the house were more ordered I would have less disordered thinking. This posturing the schism. This positioning containers.

Here is the logic I have maintained in observing my home. I spend a day of routines in roundness, comfort the tea kettle's impatient whistling. It is important to talk to objects as if they're your own. For dinner I eat a bowl of rice with raisins, but later decide that this was too much. I remove a tick of mascara suckling the corner of my eye, but later decide that this was too much. In only three hours, the bread makers will be at their routines. And from this angle, part of the angle being the sun, the town really looks quite quaint.

At the ballet, the dancers nod approvingly during one another's solos. The dancers gesture with performative arm sweeps to exclaim during others' solos. *Oh simply marvelous.*

Viewer observe. It feels like circus masters displaying the lions: *voila grand paws, voila his mane.*

It is difficult to identify a lack, hands fallen in folds of ocean, lips water between hips, this ache opening windows, my unwashed hair, the chewed ends of thumbs. But it is a skill to grow gaps, lacustrine, my voice discovered through thinking in atmospheres not scenes, through the history of a feeling.

Like a child's dull color, like a mother's shoulder blade, you believe you are building an order you resemble. You believe you are building an order you resemble to have a pair to resemble. You feel folded all over and cut by scratched lines. You are building small houses out of too-folded paper, whole villages of paper bent hard to keep standing.

Inlay the spine, gather the fingers, find thread for the ear. Build a body back to clarify: love is as much a choice as an impulse, a metal chain down a pink torn throat, a lure unhooked, the days you awake and it is not yet tomorrow. The house a feeling of a shrinking enclosure. The sink spilling. The dishes climbing. I pick my face to spit my skin

I know there is fear I know my body, a pocket unlined, a
fold now because I could not fold then.

It is important to be able to make something beautiful, to
shape it into a form even when horrifically right. There is
malevolence in misarranging information, in intentionally
throwing thoughts into wells without listening for echo.
We are built together so we break together but we must
build back together, too. If the light flickers, I flicker, too.

And it was beautiful. The night began and years passed
within the forest. Coughs of trees and the blue snow light
tapped the window. Your shape for the window. The boys
voyaged down streets. When he arrived, I let him in. I
let him slip me with his hands, knot my hair into *cheveux*,
redraw my half-opened face, move cycles of winter through
me like a train. The human formed, so belittled it remained
human, so keen in its tidy arrangement. He gathered my
skins into a skein, filled my mouth with swallows, let me
feel like I was falling into a long blue, flying unseen.

3

Elle était en train de ressembler á une petite fille, but it was not going well. She kept shifting between wolf and child, wolf, then child, her orbital eye shape pulling back and forth between angles. The dangerous ratio of muscle to bone. The circled path around the drain of the light.

It is true that in haunting, distinction between with child and with ghost is unclear, *et en train des moments de l'espace entre les deux*, she felt close to a beautiful shoulder of landscape.

Quand même, she would have preferred regularity. *La vite* threading skin. *La petite maison* settled, the moon on hill settled, the whistle white *blanche* of the neighborhood brush.

She flickered again. *Lupin.* Raked fur settled like forest inside skin. *L'enfant déchiré.* Tearing. The horror of animal when not of an animal. Untidy carnivore. Shearing of teeth. The messy detanglement *à devenir*.

The beast rose up above the table. She grew a blue tale and dove back under. She would need to find a way to escape these fixations, *á offrir l'enfant à la gueule du loup.*

4

There is a window directly across the alley from Ellis' window, and in that window there must also be a room in which a person lives, and in that room in which a person lives, that person must also be Ellis. Her lamp, too, glows yellow. Her chair, too, is red. She has yet to see a stranger at this window. She has yet to see a creature at the glass.

There is an object on the interior window sill of this room—inside the room across the alley from her—and it could be her typewriter. There is no evidence to conclude it is not.

There is a fine little blizzard at work outside their window. And the sun is setting quickly outside their window. The cat is meandering for food on her side of their window. The town hums forward as usual below.

And it is possible that the room is a room with her but a her that was herself two hours ago, the time in which she was in the other room napping or downstairs cooking or a space in which she would not frequently pass by.

Ellis is coveting their window. She is aspiring to visit. She is planning that next Tuesday she will be at the window of the window across the alley from hers when Ellis is also at mine.

5

It is unseemly to blow your nose into a tablecloth. If you share a bed with another man, keep still. If you pass a person pissing, do not greet him. Never masturbate with your bare hands. Never expose yourself unless necessary. Refrain from poking your ears while eating. If you spit, put your foot on the saliva. Do not spit so far that you have to search for the saliva.

You are exhibiting your body like an arrogant bird, pretending your wing is broken because something must be broken, with your wing freshly broken. You are hopping for display, a loon long-necked, sad and spotted all over. Your little anxious habit. Your head fully foggy. You are watching yourself watching. A mere romance of mannequin. Some social scavenger, you carver! Some desirable, you carver!

Tall fish in black dress. Ravens assembled for performative mourning. You should be thankful for your range of human emotion. You should be thankful for how much you lost in losing one another, how pout-mouthed and slouching. How ratty at the ears. What's the right word for beast when a wolf passes through? What's the right word for beast when the mountain passes through? A woman by water with her foot in dark water. The man a barracuda, she put him in braces. The bite in the bite and the matter of whom.

I step on my violin, show up to rehearsal unprepared, perform the solo in wavering wilted tones. I do not want to have given you this gift, this wealth of bereavement and petite dramas. But I carry it in parades regardless and the stretched bell stomachs of the rabbits must be cut. I am the boy who still breastfeeds in shame. I am all of my children who will never be born.

How you knew I was a stone who could be surrounded, how you curled my own body like a favorite gray mountain, how you crooned for me only like a snowy white owl. You were keeping me broken, you wanted me broken, you kept me broken to keep me here, and I performed.

And the day begins with feeling this lonely, with trying to make the sense pathological to remove my own culpability. I have been complicit with loneliness, slanted planes of light, a constant approach and readjustment of form. Do I feel lonely or do I feel pressured? Shaken face if I stay on my own. There's too much light in this room. These rooms now pull me open, carve my face with butter knives, with trees, keep me soldier for a long long time.

Fistfuls of skin, unrobe the hood. You kick at me your own dark eyes. Sometimes it is easiest to stuff my hands in my ears. Sometimes it is easiest to cut off my ears. Sometimes it is easiest to ignore my ears. But here you are—perform. I knew what it is to hold the edge of another's soft cheek, to find another thumb near to mine. We moved in a wildness of skin with your curled hair in my curled fist, the snarling animal a hand that lifted me and left.

6

There's some thunder rumbling on the hill at the top of our neighborhood and my brother says he's gonna pull his bike out of the garage and bike up and see it, say hi. I'm trying to explain that what if it's a car or a truck or a stranger we can't anticipate, standing up there at the top of the hill, glaring deep down, and when you come biking up and your legs are all tired and your arms looking small if it's a car or a truck or a stranger an unknown they'll knock you down they'll knock you all the way back down to skid the road to scrape your knees, get trapped in the sewer and get the dog barking to call such attention. *We can't risk it*, I explain. *But what if it's really thunder*, asks my brother. *We can't risk it*, I explain.

A thin-limbed fox shadows down the edge of the lane, shadowing its edge, lining its edge with a different angle. In different light, the fox becomes a fine arrangement of skin unfolded by needle, the thin-threaded face becoming before the body, the face draped back like purple cloth to expose the nose, the nose now unraveled, then the body unraveled too.

My mother spends the summer I am born digging pebbles and snails out of our garden, which she then rolls in her palms and tips easily into jars. She carves holes through the centers of each bead body and pulls them into a strand. My first birthday, she threads the string into a spine and wraps the gift in tissue paper. When worn, the snails and pebbles press into my body, and I, too, can arch my back.

And chase the dogs up the street with our armfuls. And roll the hillside downward as boxes. And label small ticks on the kitchen door frame. The coat stand like a young giraffe leaning. The basement drawing of a blurry baboon. That a disorder develops to cover disorder. That I keep trying to fill the empty room. The soft cats leaping at any affection, to be touched to be licked to be held, you reach out your arms.

Do you pull in or do you pull out? It does get easier to live with a body, to live in a body, to live with this body. Because that's what a home looks like: it has been lived in and loved a long time. Designing a home seems to require faith that you will know when you have arranged the home correctly. In the dark, sitting at the windows, I keep the interior of the turning body in this turning light.

In your quiet, I see your pity sleeping dull like a dog at your feet. Bolder the jaw. Kick knuckles to teeth. Pull out your voice and throw it to the wall, hope it sticks, doesn't slide like a squid, in the physical act of gazing, skin me bare.

I approach and notice I have the bright noise splits and what we call the bodily animal: the line between reportage and poetry when we feel the impetus for such required distinction. Dark headed the fold, a horse on my shoulders, her body skin like a tarp over metal folding chairs. No feet, like a shadow, no feet, like a sword, no feet.

I've spent all day moving a hidden anxiety that I am alone in an empty house, living with furniture. I offer the green bottles a peculiar kindness and let them sleep on my windowsill. There is a peculiar kindness to let an object sleep on your windowsill. I pretend France lives outside my window. There is a church clock bell in town that, when it rings, feels like home.

Some kids thought it'd be a neat trick to lean on my door buzzer until I answered. And I did answer, and they ran out the lobby door, giggling.

It is hard to face lights in a white-walled room. I am easing an impulse here by closing my eyes.

And how is the body now? A cold blue, driving back in snow.

Water on the road throws light I don't need. All lights seem like they're my flashing body. All lights warn I'm driving distracted of light when driving at night.

I fall on the floor at the gaze of a photograph I carried home from France and framed in our hallway.

Because I found it with love. Because I gave it with love.

Square mouthed crying the top of the stairs, square paned light slanting the wall. A house can be a quaint isolation when you keep everything else too still. And still we were here in these walls that we loved. You lived here I loved you I loved your body—here.

Little mouth standing the blue lipped window, little mouth held by the back of your hand. Diligently cleaning the skin of your shoulders, I turn and ask: did you love me before? And your angling ears. Your small gape mouth. Your round brown eyes, your beautiful eyes, they hold your face, they hold your whole face in fear.

It was a simple matter of form—a task to find an assemblage that did not require so much sincere connection, so much watching the sun gather together, so much feeling of air. But how wet bird displaying by the drain pipe, how husking tulips over the sink. We're all carrying disgust at our own corporeality but still have to carry it forward.

My grief like birds in your lap, my grief like birds nesting beaks on your shoulders. My voice flung to the wall like a ghost. Of course a month goes quickly, it's only four weeks.

All your monstering crumbled to a moment because you could not anticipate the difficulty to stand lies to a body you accidentally grew to love, the amount of will needed to walk dull-faced.

But in the end we're only looking at one another and that's all we get, the dull-faced and walking, the admission of fragmentation, a pang to find the right answer, as if there's an answer to the right thing to be.

For your answer to my question, you face me as an object, your face as a stranger in the other car's window, the soft architecture of you bent into an acted look of pain. My owl-faced boy, his eyes above—I could always tell by the intimacy of his hands how knit with worry we could be.

Along the shores of the sea-lakes, it was normal to be forgotten. Along the shores of the sea-lakes, the town looked like a girl's crooked nose.

Along the shores of the sea-lakes, the wall ran the curve of a little salting hill. Along the shores of the sea-lakes, the birds knew of the stones below the trees.

Along the shores of the sea-lakes, the crowds comforted their bodies with the rage of a creature. Along the shores of the sea-lakes, the priest fell in love with broken things as well as objects.

Along the shores of the sea-lakes, the butchers rinsed stench of their growing gently thin. Along the shores of the sea-lakes, the man envisioned a god in his own cold hands.

Along the shores of the sea-lakes, a boy pulled his boat to touch the water, it touched the water, and the water touched back.

9

Ellis believes that those on the other side of her window do not know when they have been seen, and so she stays at the window, beloved of window, watching.

To know and to care, we understand, are not the same act, different black gloves for different untidy hands. Ellis, the eye embraces, the eye can curl, the eye sweeps in-between all a body's skins.

But still, Ellis watches the neighbor shovel his sidewalk. He shuffles the snow off the sidewalk, he shuffles the snow on the sidewalk, where does it go?

Ellis learns how to carve a lucky rabbit's foot, how to pull the blade with her thumb and then smoothly click the cut, bone undone, and place the blade inside her pocket. What other items go inside a pocket?

A sister's lint pockets. A mother's clean pockets. Ellis' own dirt crumbed pockets. Ellis, walking with forest. Ellis, in a forest of shadow. Ellis, a forest of gray ravens' shadows. To look out, I look out.

10

In the selkie story, the woman is beautiful, but I am not the girl with the beautiful hair. A selkie is a seal whose whiskers you love. A selkie is a cream poured body set in a mold like a soap bar. A selkie is when gaps in the body grow lacustrine. A selkie is a body who remembers. A selkie is her background body, and what the body knows, and when it knows more than her. A selkie is a forgotten body you will find again.

Small handed, a wound slept wet like a child in my lap. Still wet in this turning, I built a body like a child who is folding, who is lived as an image of a man's quick hands, little hands in her lap, little salt in her pail, little body oh the body I formed.

You pulled the sheet away and there I was, still pretending to sleep, a bit cold, but I had known the illusion would be ending soon. It's easy to see the bat once you're out of the cave. All the scraps arranged into some kind of holy understating.

If the act of viewing gains enough density, it becomes a location. It bruises me, it is poignant to me. If it isn't an anxiety then it is a belief. I bend my body for every corner, for it isn't the leaping so much as the landing. The body works hard to prepare a divine site, to convince you to believe we are born arboreal.

And it does happen—gazed lewdly then lovely, a body can turn beautiful by passing through another's eye. Oiled with looks, the body leaves gleaming and slick, happily sexed, but as often a gaze can sicken and run like piss down a leg to dry sticky. Mostly I just get sticky.

Lately, I've been a wooden frame of an animal. I don't want this light. I keep my skin to myself to keep the gaze between my skin and me, folded safely away, an old family quilt. I don't have to feel. I don't have to cull the water. But my body assumes it takes an arrogance to know what it wants.

You have sickened me a creature, a season of trauma that has deemed me ready to recognize what is mine and what must hold in blue bottled light, that darks at windows, that speaks a cold. Do you see the window? Can you allow the window, to fold you in, in a soft light, in a soft home. You touched my grieving creature for slimed emotion. You slipped me like liquid. You slipped me like salt.

Standing over the sink husking the tulips, I don't know how to shape these days spent looking out windows. I believe in the skill to take in knowledge with care, practice domestic refining, muscle through to a kinder narrative. It is a skill to speak of a home with love, to report of love a home has witnessed. But explain, too, this pulled silence, this dampened quiet, this unspoken crumbling into blue, the flowers now crinkled.

A lady next to me on the plane moves her hand to adjust her seat strap and I instantly beat anxious at the misperception: there is a hand jacking off someone's body sitting close to me. I've seen the fluorescent computer screen too many times, a body reaching over me to feel a pink tit.

And walking through town, I clutch my arms across my chest. I tape my tits down, wear multiple camisoles, extra sweaters. Run across the gym with three shirts and taped tits. Ride the bus with two shirts and taped tits. Return home to scratch up my body and rage at its growths. And the mind is very willing to mistake correlation for connection if it appears to add order and control to the world's pattern. The bear lies before the hunter like a mere pet, lets her body relish the knife and the knife is gliding, she is gentle, she accepts the rudeness of her own brown fur.

I was uneasy, anxious, did not listen to my body. I ignored the body, it became *the* body. My body became the boy who cried wolf. Easily, the world grows overwhelming, standing on edge, screaming. And pretending is good enough, I say. It has to be, I say. Don't try so hard. Don't stand so straight. It takes my greatest strength to speak at all plainly.

See how the shadow speaks upon the wall, like a sea-creature seen swimming through a dark lens, crawling. See how the shadow speaks in the mobile's turning, how the sculpture is the summation of the turning. The sculpture is the experience of the motion of the mobile construction and the mobile shadow pulling the room together. Sometimes an object is as much its shadow as its object alone.

Calder worked with a vocabulary of shapes. He was an expert geographer. The same oval curve appears again and again across his mobiles and constructions. This time, it is translated into a new color, this time a smaller size, this time a different juxtaposition. The oval curve beside the triangle is not the same object as the oval curve behind the triangle. An oval may sleep behind a triangle and this is not the same as standing behind the triangle. The red triangle is not the same object as the blue.

I feel my body turn like a sloping, my hips cast shadows and grow eyelets, aloft. In air I am subject to current and turn like a liquid, my motion and spinning pull in the room and the shadowed together. It speaks again, it speaks of me. I am red form gazing, red jawed walking, angled deeply, as skin, as sea.

11

We step outside and there's an uneasiness. The birds are shuffling their arms inside their wings. A dog passes with a raw umber underbelly and I give a small garden stone a second take, but we keep walking. Reach a street corner and don't know what to do with our hands while the light takes forever to change. Pass a yellow sign that warns us of gusty winds, but only maybe. Feel a depth well in our mouths, find a language before we know what it's for. I hold such fear in my shoulders and today we're oddly bodied. There's progress here I'm sure, but it can be hard to tell.

If we're hunting gazelle, what does poetry get to be? The fear shattered okapi, the fur puffed doe, the russet color of a quick coati coat? Re-adjust your arms inside your sleeves. Reach your wrists for your pockets. Watch a sparrow on the edge of the little salting hill. You can't jump in red tusked and fighting, demand animal ordinal rearrangement, like a brute, rush the prey, you know nothing of leaping.

I have been thinking on rabbits, the air they hold inside their fur. Are there stories written about rabbits without trembling? Rabbit stone in the field, do you see me? As a rabbit, you have marvelous ears. As a rabbit, you have particularities about cleanliness. Living this world is easier when you are here with me. I'm finding it's quite hard to ever get away from you being you. If I am mad, how do we decide I am so? Not the thing but the thing itself. Tuffed up, tuffed up high, and you are a rabbit light. If a film is the movement between the flickering, is a rabbit anything at all?

The real question is this: when you die, will you have written all the rabbit fables you intended? You must think ambitiously and hope for many rabbit fables. In giving yourself many rabbits, you gift yourself a kindness. Do not worry about how to justify the fables. Do not worry about how to justify playfulness. Consider an array of rabbits, a rabbit as observed through a window, a rabbit as a stone, a rabbit formed for a child, a child formed for a rabbit.

Sometimes you feel truly so small, the tiniest horse in the largest of fields. Still, there is safety—the blue expander sky, the line of the mountain, your hand on the horse. In all our troubled landscape, scraps of light still case inside snow, and slanted fields still pull a rough peace towards an old bellwether, she belled and moving field through the field into trees. To gaze the snow, to look out encased and coveted, the snow hung light.

At the piano, the lift from a note to a rest is as much the architecture of music as the lift from a note to a note. Examine Chopin. Examine Satie. Feel the length run down the bottom of the arm. The rest that follows a note forms the note's shadow. You cannot lilt, you cannot arc emotion, you cannot dip into sound unless you allow yourself time to move through the air and shadow.

Nijinsky understood that the body's imagined relationship to space is as important to our understanding of ourselves as the body's real relationship to space. Nijinsky could not simply feel light—feel light with conviction, and then float with ease. A dancer's body takes muscle and bend and bending. A dancer's body must be broken before it can be reborn. To hold the air takes all your power! Still, the imagined space of the body is real and its power is real. Nobody who attended a Nijinsky performance could be convinced otherwise. Leaving the theater, they would gasp that they had seen an angel. Gravity no longer felt so dense. The body had been given permission to leave its daily routine. Their own person may now move through their world at a new angle, with new lift. The impact of the imagined is all we ask.

At the sound of an evening shuffling, I should not have to fear a gaze. Who was permitting? Who was responsible? One of us reached, and I only remember turning. In love I grew like a child's thin figure, the red swallow's nest, your summer evening, we built a swing. But who was complicit, and when was the turning, and what do you think of the word beloved, which contains a nobility love does not require?

If there were two, we needed to reach assent together. But how do you gather language for a concept you do not yet know to see? You must build a container around a fluid to feel a cage. I understood enough to believe that my body feels like a hand has reached through into my chest, turning cathedral white fingers. It lurked between my ribs, brushed my lung while passing through. You fear a stranger watching you sleep, but understand this: the stranger is you.

Black and white film keeps a flickering in-between, keeps a flickering in-between my bodies. Remember the importance of light and the greater importance of its absence. I pour a bath in which to sit my sleep, let the porcelain light circle the thick mouths of the faucet and drain, soothed. It is difficult to be able to identify a lack. *There must be words for what is not there.* In the case of a ladder, a shadow is not as much the ladder as the object itself. You cannot climb a shadow.

On the page you seem so quiet. I can pass through all your vowels and consonants without sticking. I can touch all your words without thinking to stop. I build a mesh screen for you to pass through, for me to assess you. You oblige and walk. Let me move gentle through your hair and pooled skin. I manage to collect a half light, a dirty silver, only the dust of a dusty light. What does this mean, you ask. I ask you to pass through the screen more loudly. You tell me you are louder. I tell you that you will have to rage a little more dramatically. Ignite a fire, I say. Burn a church, I say. Consider damnation. You tell me that you are raging, that you have, that you do, that consider the shape of your rage is not of my own.

My understanding was that I was simply to react provocatively when played upon. Now, my body is fresh like a violin. I want to feel and then be peeled like an orange, unrobed by strong nails, rolled across tables full of scent in my skin, plump, thick. I want to be ground against the wire of my strings, pressed pressed and grated like the cinnamon peeler, slips of peel and heady with scent. I run up the strings. I knot the string. I used to know my wrists of birds, the thoughts you loved but could not order.

It will have been everything and I will have lost it. Bodies kept to craving and impeded by longer nail, rough intimacy, my head a stranger's, your stallion, bleating skin thick as March. Eyes shut the light closing, eyes shut the door closing. Mother mother this knowing. And mother mother this door. We loved the way a family fills with light like a body as a container you must keep to keep going.

Within the forest, I read all desire as assault, all flocks of birds as leaping hands, all hands: the creation of hands. The trees are high, crested. The snow collects in the crooks of the trees. I navigate a crest of ferns. I lift my legs. There are many ways to desire, and many ways to own an object. But the ground below is only pulling forward. I stay motionless, the surroundings they turn below me. Wave to the observer above.

It was a compulsion, a pulled unavoidable act. The creature on the dais in the center of the room a monster, say creature, say it was a creature: he saw me exposed and skinned my chest open, my body lying on the ground, his eyes above. He could have looked into the into of my body. He could have held the into of my body. He could have could peer, he could he my body, you had to lie on your back to feel any ability to speak the room.

12

Slowly, you are learning this gray dulling April. You are learning patience for cold. You are learning that snails may sleep in snow mounds to maintain solid interiority. You practice your snail pose for weeks under your bed covers, now musty from all your night sweats. You practice curling more tightly to maintain interiority. If sleep keeps your eyes closed, further stimuli cannot be entered into the system. You are learning how to manage the stimuli in your system. Keep new stimuli out of the system.

Snow leopard: *Panthera uncia*. *Panthera* on the resemblance of cranial features. The dorsal profile of the skull tolerably convex, the basicranial axis horizontal, the convexly rounded chin sloping. *Panthera*. *Pantherinae*, a subfamily first named and described in 1917. *Panthera*. The absence of a snow leopard roar, it was assumed, was because of the incomplete ossification of the snow leopard's hyoid bone. *Panthera*. *Panthera*, *Pantherinae*, then *Felidae*. The snowy leopard, properly referred to as the snow leopard, properly referred to as *Panthera uncia*. *Felidae*. Study the mammal encyclopedia to select your large *Felidae* species. My brother claimed a jaguar. I loved a snow leopard. *Felidae*. *Felidae*, a lineage of carnivores with gracile and muscular bodies. *Felidae*, originating in Asia and spreading across continents through land bridges. *Felidae*, when your coat becomes a pelt. *Felidae*, then *Carnivora*, where-in creatures have large teeth and claws for flesh. The better to eat you with my pretty. The better to see you with my pretty.

The wallaby stuffed animal creature is not recommended for cradling. He has sharp and inflexible leather nails and ears, has been over stuffed, could be used as a small brick. The wallaby stuffed animal creature: may be used as a presence against the small of a back to protect the child from wandering fear that larger and less predictable creatures will enter their room at night. Children learn to fear feeding creatures one way or another, but the wallaby helps delay exposure. The wallaby stuffed animal creature. We do not believe in exposure therapy.

You learn early that you can kill ants if you gaze them deeply through a lens darkly slanted. Gaze and observe, but not so sharply that the sun focuses or angles towards destruction. Squint if necessary. Shade your eyes if necessary. Do not look at all if necessary. If you gaze, gaze gently. Those of us gazed learn most quickly to be more gentle gazers. Those of us rarely under the knife are often unaware of our own carving power.

She has dissected a cow's eye. She has sliced it like an egg. She has scraped away its iris. The texture is resistant, rubbery in resistance. She has written reports on distinctions between the eyes of octopuses and giant squids. Phylum *Mollusca* of the invertebrates. Phylum *Chordata* of the human eye, the vertebrates, the lemur. Phylum *Chordata* the vertebrates the fish eye. Phylum *Chordata* the vertebrates. Giant squids have the largest eye of all creatures. Invertebrates vastly outnumber chordates. The human eye is disappointingly flimsy in its visual spectrum range.

I learn the desire to make houses out of sticks and stairs out of stone with my own calloused hands. I build the desire to build a nest, and I build my home. Abalone is pronounced with both hard 'o' and 'e.' Abalone are edible mollusca of warm seas. Abalone are pierced with respiratory holes. My breathing is not pierced with respiratory holes. I am not pneumostomed. I can carry air much further distances. Seals may eat pneumostomed creatures if water temperatures sort conveniently. Most often, however, if an abalone is eaten by a mammal, the mammal will be an otter.

I ask my father the biologist to classify our family members within the taxonomic family systems *Bovidae* and *Cervidae*.

We are standing beside a taxidermied okapi within the Natural History Museum in Washington, D.C. My father takes several minutes to reflect. I leave his side to explore the other taxidermies: one of the last tasmanian devils, a pangolin, a tenrec, a mountain goat leaping from a tan mountain lion. As a child on family walks through the forest, my parents would call me their little mountain goat. I return to my father's side. My mother is an antelope. My father is a water buffalo. My brother is not named. I am a dik dik, and the identification as such a petite hoofed creature signifies that I am greatly loved.

13

My vibrato fingers, my piano hands—forgive me my neglected musician's body. I opened my violin case for the first time today in five years and found inside the curled body of a tiny child sleeping. I don't know when he crawled into this womb. He seems to have been waiting for me for quite a long time. Toed feet, suckle fist, he's lying as if in one of those holy cradles that washes up on shores.

I hold the child to my chin as I would my violin, tuck him under the dip of my neck. Let him breathe the same skin folds. I'm already skeptical of the fit of the body to the body. And to care for anything built out of a jumbled skin skeleton. But the history of a child is a history of a body. I am a seedling now, thrown in a river.

I mourn for the missing body of my beloved instrument. His surely broken strings. His loosened peg posts. The child sleeps the red velvet violin case. I rosin his nails, attach the metronome to his chest like a bomb. I want to spittle his chin.

And now I've been living with this moon faced creature, this owler at my elbow, for the past several months. He's performing in corners. He's emerging in armfuls. My instincts tell me I am about to enter a period of great production. Did I then produce this child? The child grows in bursts in the slants of the hallways. The child scrawls a body and I feel outliered.

The child a rabid ivy vine. The child in my shaking. The child a mirror at all of my edges.

The light bulbs sit tidy in their wire housing structures. I take to sliding the slants of the white glaring walls. The cherry blossoms blooming, then blowing. Full swirls down empty rain streets. Silver light in the rain, they billowed near me; I thought they were snow.

14

Not recognizing my personhood has been problematic to me in the past, but my savagery is genderless and sleeps my body into exhaustion. My flaws are in not embracing, but also in not embracing adherence. Not everything we touch must touch the high holy. Not all nights are undrugged sleep. Bathing is a way to feel small inside a soap dish. Bathing is a way to practice your folding.

I find an owl in the yard with souring feather and wipe the sweat away from his lip. I move forward. Drag my feet against the path. Leave my shadow draped across a bed of branches. If I leap, I leap tall, I leap tall as an arm, my weight above. The white wall flies to the ceiling unstopped. Sometimes the story burrows ahead, growling. Sometimes it rushes bedside eager to pray.

A sweet little savagery, he tells me, you exhibit, my lips licked. I leave my gloves folded tidy at the edge of the sink, turn to face him. There's a too large dose of his first person crowding my consciousness lately. It is a bizarre little body, but we keep it as a specimen, a lab rat pet. And what is a speed of want?

She builds a ladder from the roof, climbs the sky like a bird. But have you heard of a bird needing a step stool, slowly the spilling swallows: torsos reared, mouths ready to bite, it's feeling freshly horrored, it's in the dream my mouth gaping, crowding with carapace, with trees.

I pull my leaf leg stockings off my body, these white leaves tattooed twinning up my legs. Sitting on the bed in my underwear, I disgust at my body, my skin being skin and weight being weight. I fantasize a scalpel, or a pair of baby's nail scissors, to cut into this flesh, tear it out, rake an incision from my navel to my ribs.

You have to dig deep so there's enough skin to grip when you put down the scalpel to reach in and pull back, then you pin back. It's like in high school when you dissected the dogfish the frogs the pigs in biology, except here there's no rush of formaldehyde scent, only you and you and you. Reach in, pull back, stick in your nails, then tear. Grip this disgust! If it fills you do something, even if to do is to harm. Tear the skin, rip easily down your neck so your face peels in two. The tension of the scissors cutting through the thick skin is a thick resistance, satisfying beauty. You're a beauty.

I am not your darling girl with the cute red bow cheeks, priss lips, sweet head of a fucked baby doll. Can I explain the animalistic that my nails clawed into my skin, that picked into my face? You cute little toy. You paper flower all sloppy from rain. I want to spit at you this shit you swim my ear. The gushing is gross, I know, but I've been bottled. I bottled my little mouth with a twist off top shoved back on.

The stranger in my fears was me. I poemed it. I hurt you. I let you be. The same trick pulled over again. Pulled over pulled out. I was the one who wanted to bend you with my bent hand. I am the broken corner that you miss holding.

We are taught avoid the abstract: those concepts will swallow. But there is a space for sentimentality. There is a face for the sincere. I never let an approach to see how delightfully in fear I might allow consumption. Do you allow this to unfurl? Do you pin back your cheeks? Are you again a paper doll where the clothes won't pinch put?

Yes, I am here, and you—simultaneously in such aggravating logic, my own confused arctic landscape I cannot help but ask for once a night. You smile those rock gullies singing down your windpipe into a dark thickness. Your tongues assemble, rasp. Pour upon my shaking animal, and I am to pretend appealing. I have never been more open than during this fear it is I discovered: I had been at the mouth of a wet-lipped cave.

15

And how do I get rid of this fever? If I am going to call this tomorrow, I must get braver each time. Walking my southern shadow, the asphalt presses my bare feet. Drought green sits in the trees, the cicadas chorus, the lawn sprinklers click their rounds. There's the fireworks from the laser show in the distance, each night at seven. There's the neighbor's dog startled from the fireworks from the laser show, each night at seven.

I remember a home now dusty where I watched my grandmother's laugh fly under the dogwood tree, the dogs chase the yard in spiky grass, the hill roll in cardboard boxes, the best daffodils bloom from the home grown field. We played basketball in a gravel field. We planted a maple tree for my grandparents' anniversary. I once had to pick out my own switch from the overgrown weeds patch in that yard. I cried while sorting through the stalks. My father left before I finished my search. The search was the punishment.

And the dark-lipped window is pulling me in to this light. We are still in this grieving, we are still holding to this grieving. The stone rabbit guarding the front porch stairs, the gray cat licking the back of my thumb, the condensation fogging the glass porch windows. If we don't rearrange the furniture, are we hoping that some sort of life will resume, resprout like weeds in an untended garden? All edges painted, marked, placed. Do we need the mourning to hold us because we do not know how to hold one another?

My grandmother's laugh flies under the dogwood tree. Billow me, pretend there is more. Sometimes I remember that a life contains an awful lot of moments, but I do not have to live them all. We slip in and out with our watery body. To catch everything would be awing but only briefly.

The sky is not yet finished unfilling, draining towards its habit of bedtimes. I spend the hour before bed drawing cross-faced rabbits. Drawing swan faced rabbits. Drawing swan faced not swanned faced rabbits. Porcelain faced.

Under the sweep of a southern thunderstorm, a house can swallow. When covered in rain, the carpet grows thick, the stereo a whir, notes from the piano melt cold. The air hums throughout the house and walls of glass porches fog. From inside, enveloped in cool, the house leans sleepy. Ideas muffle into the humidity and return in the dark, hours later, the storm only marked by dripping trees.

Why would a description of a rabbit be important, hold import, hold importance? Can you say with sincerity that a description of a rabbit, in written or drawn form, has not shaped you as a person? Can you say with sincerity that there are not multiple descriptions of rabbits that have shaped you as a person, inspired you to think playfully and with kindness and persistence and an openness to that which is not immediately beheld? How many people's perceptions of creatures do you need to change for your work to count as important? Three rabbits? Ten? Can the lyric alone be enough?

When I arrive home, my creature greets me at the door. She circles me twice. She shows me how well she can sharpen her nails. Sometimes I hold my creature in my arms immediately. Sometimes I search the rooms for spots of warmth to determine where my creature has been sleeping. Other times I ignore her while I unload the groceries and organize the kitchen, acting fully civilized. If I ignore my creature she takes to rumpusing the house in agitation. Jumping on tables. Emitting great yowls. It's important to acknowledge your creature. There's no escaping she's yours.

Pain is a sensitivity to the world and its chaos. This pain is a gift. It is a skill to feel, but you do not have to feel. People are sick, but don't be sicker. We will stand the room hips, our small-breasting hips. Is it satisfying enough for the rabbit to be a respite? The rabbit is a location of respite.

16

Ellis has been coveting a stone in her neighbor's front yard for some months now, but here at the dawn of October, the ice cream truck is still singing rounds outside her bedroom window, the sparrow still feeding, and the stone still untouched. Tomorrow will make three months since she began her coveting. "We're unlikely to find a better one," advises her brother, and he is right; such specimen are rare.

Each evening, Ellis and her shadow walk along the gutter of Eckerd's Lane to the warm asphalt cul-de-sac to observe the stone in neighborhood evening. It is a gray stone amongst an arrangement of mostly white stones. Bold nose, bold shoulder, thin scar skirting its back—it is easy to spot from the end of the neighbor's driveway. Each evening the fluorescence sits kindly in the trees, each night the fluorescence sits kindly, and Ellis checks on the thin scar stone. "It must be quite lonely," pressures her brother. "You should capture it soon," pressures her brother.

But Ellis has been trained as an observer, not as an enacter. How to perform a list of tools and nets required for extraction? She is exceptionally cautious about approaching the stone with an incorrect arrangement of skin. Should she approach incorrectly, the stone might grow startled and turn in character. A stone may sleep steady at the edge of the azaleas, but approached by rough boots or scrape of a trowel—the mode of acquisition is essential.

The last weekend of October, Sunday morning sunning day, Ellis ties her boots to her feet, selects a silver fishing net from the garage, and walks the gutter of Eckerd's Lane to the cul-de-sac. To sleep the lawn, to sleep the lawn gently. She steps onto the lawn.

And the old wolf saw his reflection in the local swimming pool, a small path through the woods to reach the water. The trees stood kindly in their fluorescence, their fluorescence sitting kindly in the trees.

17

It happened on a Tuesday. I entered the room and the room kept giving. I entered the world and the world kept giving. I entered the room and something looked behind. Looked behind, looked back.

I want for you a more carved language. I want for you a carving language. And the word: it was never a single object, it was never a single form. Do it larged. Do it wrought. Do it as a house dented by emotion.

The space of a room is a performance, and it's better not to be in a hurry. You get harried and besotted. Open the door. Step inside. Gaze to the ceiling. Gaze to the floor. Assess the room's breadth. Assess the room's ease. Assess the room's containers and containments. Strive for a more intimate relationship with objects. Desire a great sincerity of connection. This is not a vase, this is your mother's vase. This is not a chair, this is your father's chair. You must act the room. Spread yourself widely. Wave your arms. Wake up the air. A house can be physically wrecked by chaotic thought. Don't let the birds swoop in. Retrain your compulsions or the siding will crumble. You must hope for a simple catastrophe—all the china smashed in a single go. My sour, stabbed and splayed. Do it wrought do it right.

What does it mean to be a location? If the act of viewing itself gains enough density, it becomes a location.

Do it wrought do it right and the lyric alone will be a room still giving.

Should the collectivity of birds enter *la maison*, the *maison* will become an act of viewing: all eyes on the creatures, the creaturely, all eyes in attendance. Should the collectivity of birds enter *la maison*, the *maison* will billow, turn and dent with emotion. Shrieks will emit from the creatures viewing the creatures. Shrieks will emit from this holy act of viewing. I don't know how to relate to objects without consumption and the birds don't either. Do you have a better plan than this pecking? Shriek louder. Shriek for more indentation. Shriek for the wallpaper to finally peel.

It happened on a Tuesday. It happened on a Tuesday and I awoke panting. It happened on a Tuesday and the children were still born. It happened on a Tuesday and my neck took to aching. It happened on a Tuesday and my toes kept to pointing. I looked up and the room descended. Sleep fell like a dusting, a tossed up tent of fabric that billowed back down. Inside with the heat and the dim, the man's round face reminded me of an umbrella I once had owned.

18

And yes, I will have this act again. I will see it through like a whimper, cold shoulders in the pond, its scent decomposing too strongly odored like a fox, this flesh, unruly. Quick body in the turn, the downstream current, *l'oiseau qui chante. Le bruit qui chante*, reopen the window, this light, *l'oiseau*, and the tilt, *à gauche*, like a folding, the trees, fluorescent, craned necks, like a wailing of ghost, this light of skin.

Yesterday I saw my home running through someone else's dream, absconding from me like a rude mockingbird. She wore stilt legs, long tights, was flipping her skirt as she went along.

And sometimes being human feels like wrapping pink twine around a bold wolf's ear, knotting his wheat fur, combing his tail. Where to even place your hands when near his back? How to avoid hesitation to assert hierarchy? I check the pelvis for fleas and the muzzle bites back. Bad mouth like a bird I try to pin better. I swallow, smile docile, the crane who can't fly.

Pussyfooting: because your cock comes first. Pussyfooting: because everyone else is broken. Pussyfooting: because your erection is hurting. Pussyfooting: because your partner must be interested. Pussyfooting: because what other choice did you have.

Mother says to stay proper but I keep spilling my skirt. The blond sheep bleat red before I noticed her wool. The baker had to scold before I stole loaves of bread. The subway had to break down nine times before I began to slip my hands into people's back pockets—but how I loved my hands once they were there.

When I ask am I creaturial I ask was my mother creature, too. Did she dream of fish leaving the aquarium, the terrarium walls melting, falling at our feet puddled and swim?

Sometimes the cock is a quick bird I try to catch with my hands, but end up fumbling on my blouse instead. You have to practice practice the soft pulling pink. Nurture your nails to fine tune the wrist. My hand's a bent corner. My hand's a violin. Come now controlled, let loose now the yarn.

It took me years to build into this wild. Whole lineages of growth, little bean poles tangling. Intimacy of the okapi, intimacy of the polar bear. My body never stood a chance at independence, we were curdled before born.

We'll never live without our mothers, the way they thread our spines shaping the arches of our backs, our verbed necks, lifted arm lifted shoulder. I hold such fear in my shoulders so I'll carry that forward.

And why is restraint seen as so wholly unwanted? Jawlines to angle, the brows now to bold. Make the mouth a tight soldier, but let her be coy.

I watched how he climbed each rung of her body, how he praised her borrowed skin. The cicadas crawling up my arms to my ears. Suckling, they hang like wet leaves. Even interiority grows crowded. It's like standing on the edge; you start looking all around.

This is my body after the storm, backwash green, mildew and blue. My lips smile with whittle teeth. My legs like wooden toys. Skinned feet like a lamb. A blind felt piglet. In french, the words for smile and mouse brush shoulders. Mother tells me better face the wolf than your own accord, better make a list than face the wolf, better remember the thread from your wrist to his ear.

19

The rabbit is at the window, ruffling. The rabbit is tending her ankles and shoulder blades as most creatures cannot. The rabbit is scratching her back with her own back leg. In living in this home, she will become a catalog of household objects and descriptors. In living, she will be described.

The rabbit has a fixation with the closet door. At each hourly house rotation, the rabbit enters the upstairs bedroom, skirts the edge of the bed, and rushes to push her nose against the gap between the closet door and its door frame. Each rotation, the rabbit sits for thirty seconds in front of the bedroom's one closet door. She might place a white paw on the crack of the frame. She might stretch her torso to reach the doorknob. She might retreat several paces to the other side of the red dresser to peer at the door from around a barrier. Often she might sharpen her ears towards potential alarm coming from the brown closet door.

If the door is opened, as it occasionally is for the home's resident to retrieve coats and collars, the rabbit will rush to the vicinity. The rabbit is not shy about making her interest in the closet door known. The home resident knows of the rabbit's interest. If the closet door is opened, the rabbit will, if lucky and swift-bodied, slip inside. Sometimes the home resident intentionally leaves the door ajar so as to watch the creature slip inside. Sometimes the creature is faster than the home resident would like. Sometimes the creature is accidentally locked inside the closet.

But once inside, there is hardly anything to explore. The carpet has a bit of a musty odor. The hanging coats smell like the home resident. There is a bit of laundry detergent scent from old blankets. It used to be that the floor of the closet included space for rabbit nesting, circling, exploring. The home resident has since moved many oddities into the closet, crowding the floor space. Boxes of unread books. Domino and card games for festivities with friends the home resident no longer has. The home resident could be filled with greater decency, could move her collection of nonsense to another room. The closet room is of great importance.

Still, despite the seeming lack of attractions, the rabbit maintains a steady interest in the room behind the bedroom closet door. Weeks have passed, months, a year. Perhaps the home resident at one point considered this interest a simple phase to be worked through, to move on from, matured. But it is not so. Every hourly house rotation, the rabbit visits the bedroom closet door.

20

Sewn into the age of light, we drew the sun up each morning from the well and bathed our feet in her lips, sank our shoulders to feel our body arches. Each night our world billowed up like a tent to wrap inward, skyward, slipped off all the knots. And each following morning we would retether the world to our images, pull the sky down like a kite, pull her fingers back into our mouths.

Tether the sky at the apple tree, tether the sky at the storm drain. The sky tethered to the laundry. The sky tethered to the hedgerow. And yes the best we could manage was to tuck the images into place, not sew them like a stronghold. We practiced with fitted bedsheets.

Sometimes images became mismatched and we were left with odd happenings. There was the day we slept late and the apple tree fell. There was the day my father's hand snagged in sky fabric, the barn roof flew away, lifted open like a hat. The untethering a process like a holy renaming— thee frog you are free, thee rose you are free.

It's not that when images were untethered they disappeared, but their particularity blurred. They became gathered, lightly tangled. Bathed in the wash, the mind could curl around their leftover light, in a turning, the face, pulled left—

Many animals would appear promptly for their nightly naming. The rabbit as a stone in the field, the deer's eyes as soft quiet in the woods. And you could feel the untethering at dusk quite naturally, a blurriness settling in, ensembles of images.

Sometimes the image was a little too darling and we were handed a rough needle: my rabbit's tail unspooled, like an arm, this humidity. Morning image overlap: the dove as your left shoulder, the okapi as your next kin. Sew our shadows our stockings. Consider her an unsorted whole.

Sewn into the age of light, we were required each morning to reinvent reasons for our existence, to justify our own imaging. If you felt a bit peculiar mid-morning, it was likely your own skin.

21

We brush our snarling hair. We sleep in sweaty curls. We are carried as a child. We are held in others' arms. We know more of the mammal than we know of our own. Our mother ties her shoes. Our father knots his tie. Our parents stand touching, together, in the garden, conferring. They will not touch us. We will sew our skin together with needle and thread.

Her round back, her oval back, like a cream colored egg speckled in brown. She breathes in the bath and her breasts dip and peak, legs lean against the walls, her feet chase the soap across the tub bottom.

We learn our bodies when we fall asleep on stranger's shoulders, get shoved on swings, sleep beside a stranger in guilt, sleep with a friend in quiet. When words are chosen carefully. When our family language is architectural and our body emulates. We learn our bodies when we hear people outside our window on wet Friday nights.

My mother taught me early that one day somebody I love dearly will leave me. *You bitch,* she said. *You bitch,* she said crying.

My brother once told me that I am not ugly, but definitely not beautiful. My mother touches my hair and frowns. My father whispers that I smell. A friend lets me know I'm not one of the attractive ones. A love says I am kidding if I think I'll find better.

I grew my shoulder blades from my back like elk grow their antlers. I tightened my spine straight with ivory. I stained my skin red from eating tomatoes. I whittled my teeth from pottery shards. My lips, they formed naturally when my body learned joy.

I show my mother a picture of my recent weekend trip. She says *you look pretty, and you look happy.* My father expresses he is happy I am home. He says *you look so pretty.* My grandmother loves me. She says *you are the girl with the beautiful hair.* But I am not the girl with the beautiful hair. My nails are claws. I've sucked a cunt. I don't believe in hell. I am my own sweetest leaper.

My darling, I've always wanted. And this isn't anxiety, this is belief. Let the children's coats be so dirty the sky

stays standing inside their sleeves. Let the mouth stand as
a warm tempting interior. Make me a raven with brambles
wreathed around his neck. An umbrella walked through
the storm of blue.

You loved me as the girl with freckles up her sleeves, and it
might be true that in loving one thing you lose another. But
it is fall now, trees blooming, outside the window whole
tangles of branches, whole screams of branches, whole
possibilities of wholly separate allotments of skin.

And we were, the lion eating her hand full but gentle. The
sun showing her shoulders to winter rehemming. Pink on
my shoulders. My papa sharpening all the kitchen knives.
My mother sitting watching our battle routines. What
delicacies these rocks! What branches these hips! The
views displayed in light so human.

Gazed through the bedroom window, the rabbit with a
gentle leaning towards the field of movement and blurr.
The sun pulls a fur weight in light soft light soft home
round quiet across the gray light passing into your perch

at the window. And quiet to gaze and discover a small body beholden but distant from you by glass.

In longing, it is painful to gaze through a window a rabbit's and your separation, to allow the rabbit anonymity to yours with slant, a gentle leaning towards the field through its unbeheld indent. The rabbit grown gazed and longer in longing now yours your own. Rabbit dear of wilderness indent beheld and beloved. For you must let her sleep this green field alone.

Notes

Section 5

Stanza one is a compilation of adapted quotes from Norbert Elias' *The Civilizing Process.*

Section 8

"Along the shores of the sea-lakes" is a phrase from H.D.'s *Notes on Thought and Vision.*

Section 11

This section uses language inspired by Wallace Stevens' poem "A Rabbit as King of the Ghosts." The phrase "There must be words for what is not there" is a play on a line from Dara Wier's poem "An Ant in the Mouth of the Furnace."

Section 12

Moments of language about snow-leopards were inspired by language from *Fauna of British India Mammalia Volume 1* (second edition) (Reginald Innes Pocock), "On the Tooth-change, Cranial Characters, and Classification of the Snow-Leopard or Ounce (Felis uncia)" (Reginald Innes Pocock), and "Hyoid structure, laryngeal anatomy, and vocalization in felids (Mammalia: Carnivora: Felidae)" (G. Peters & M.H. Hast).

Acknowledgements

With waves of gratitude, thanks in abundance—

To the editors and readers of the following journals, in which excerpts of *The Girl Who Became a Rabbit* first appeared: *Bennington Review, Black Warrior Review: Boyfriend Village, The Boiler, Copper Nickel, Cream City Review, Denver Quarterly, Figure 1, Michigan Quarterly Review, The Offing, Passages North, The Seventh Wave, Southern Humanities Review, The Spectacle: The Revue, Trestle Ties, Tupelo Quarterly, and Yalobusha Review.*

To the visual artists who have unknowingly joined me at the writing table and guided me in building the atmospheric theaters of *Rabbit.* "Be playful, be wilder," you whispered: Etel Adnan, Hilma Af Klint, Beatrice Alemagna, Louise Bourgeois, Henry Darger, Alexander Calder, Alexis Callender, Alois Cariget, Leonora Carrington, Joanna Concejo, Emily Dickinson's envelopes, Ian Felice, Ellen Gallagher, Renee Gladman, Edward Gorey, Allison Janae Hamilton, Sarah Jarrett, YunKyung Jeong, Graciela Iturbide, Nahid Kazemi, Davood Koochaki, Violeta Lópiz, Vivian Maier, Jackie Morris, Kay Nielsen, Beatrix Potter, Lorna Simpson, Peter Sís, Kiki Smith, Bianca Stone, Pamela Phatsimo Sunstrum, Javier Téllez, Bill Traylor, Cy Twombly, Monika Vaicenaviciene, Sandra Vásquez de la Horra, Tetsuhiro Wakabayashi, Kara Walker, Issa Watanabe, Francesca Woodman, and Lisbeth Zwerger.

To my early creative instructors. To Kathy Stewart, whose music I do not forget. To Mary Lynn Huie, for all the after school writing sessions and letting me slip under her wing. To Dan Chiasson, who found and encouraged shape within the notes for poems.

To the University of Massachusetts Amherst MFA community and Tin House Summer Workshop for dedicated writing time and invaluable feedback. To Peter Gizzi and Ocean Vuong for their mentorship in how to love poetry and their sharp edits. To Dara Barrois/Dixon, who first saw and championed the roots of this book when I was about to toss it, who pushes me to grow into myself and my voice.

To *The Seventh Wave* family, particularly Joyce Chen and Bretty Rawson, who help me find community and joy within the world of literary publishing.

To the dear hearts and steadiness and love of Ell Davis, Maggie Foley, Mark Mangelsdorf, and Alyx Raz; Animal Club; my Wellesley (and Wellesley-in-Aix) champions

Kristina Bracero, Ali Fisher, Kellen Kartub, Smaranda Sandu, Laura Yan, Claire Gulliver, Mary French, Dan Kirby, and Elizabeth Blackwell; Rob Strain, who was at ground zero; Amanda Dahill-Moore, for countless hours at her kitchen table and unwavering gentle guidance; and Rebecca Valley, great coyote, there for all seasons of wind and rain, pastries and puppet shows.

To Julia Menzel, my first reader and first friend. You are loved and loving, always, but particularly during our kitchen clean-up dances. To my grandparents, my early and constant poetry advocates who taught me the foundational writing principle of good food and good story around a wooden table. To my dear Brent Cornelius. You are the kindest person I know. To be fiercely loved not in spite of but for our oddities and wildness—you every day offer and teach me this rarest gift.

To my father, Charles Menzel, who showed me how to properly approach animals, to see and adore their quick shifts in character, who imbued "the importance of describing phenomena, of not assuming that things already have been well described, and of checking what lies behind verbal labels and attractive conclusions."

To my mother, Jane Gagné, who taught me how and why to build a creative life, who first trained me on the art of the line, whose care and curiosity I carry forward. There are no color fields I love as much as yours.

And to all my dear ones who report their sightings of rabbits in fields, who helped seeing a rabbit became an event, then an encounter, a small myth.

HUB CITY PRESS

PUBLISHING
New & Extraordinary
VOICES FROM THE
AMERICAN SOUTH

HUB CITY PRESS is a non-profit independent press in Spartanburg, SC that publishes well-crafted, high-quality works by new and established authors, with an emphasis on the Southern experience. We are committed to high-caliber novels, short stories, poetry, plays, memoir, and works emphasizing regional culture and history. We are particularly interested in books with a strong sense of place.

Hub City Press is an imprint of the non-profit Hub City Writers Project, founded in 1995 to foster a sense of community through the literary arts. Our metaphor of organization purposely looks backward to the nineteenth century when Spartanburg was known as the "hub city," a place where railroads converged and departed.

The New Southern Voices Book Prize was established in 2013 and is a biennial prize awarded to an emerging Southern poet who has published at most one previous collection of poetry. It is awarded for a book-length collection of poems written originally in English.

PREVIOUS WINNERS

2021: Marlanda Dekine *Thresh & Hold*

2019: Megan Denton Ray *Mustard, Milk, and Gin*

2017: Lindsey Alexander *Rodeo in Reverse*

2015: J.K. Daniels *Wedding Pulls*

2013: Lilah Hegnauer *Pantry*

HUB CITY PRESS books are made possible through the generous support of grants and donations from corporations, state and federal grant programs, family foundations, and the many individuals who support our mission of building a more inclusive literary arts culture, in particular: Byron Morris and Deborah McAbee, Charles and Katherine Frazier, and Michel and Eliot Stone. Hub City Press gratefully acknowledges support from the National Endowment for the Arts, the Amazon Literary Partnership, the South Carolina Arts Commission, the Chapman Cultural Center, Spartanburg County Public Library, and the City of Spartanburg.